THE TEACHING OF ENGLISH GRAMMAR

IN considering the use of any branch as a subject of study in schools, the first question is, Why study it at all? Of what use is it? Why, then, have we by common consent introduced grammar into our courses of study? The answer to this question is threefold. We study grammar because a knowledge of sentence-structure is an aid in the interpretation of literature; because continual dealing with sentences influences the student to form better sentences in his own composition; and because grammar is the best subject in our course of study for the development of reasoning power.

Literature is the expression of the thoughts of great men. These thoughts are expressed in sentences. As the thoughts grow in complexity, the expression becomes more involved. Yet in all the intricacies of the most involved thought, there are somewhere to be found the simple elements of every sentence. When these are surely known in their mutual relations, the rest of the thought falls very easily into its proper place. Now why can the grammar-trained pupil unravel intricate thoughts more easily than the child untrained in grammar?

Simply because he has been studying thought-expression all the time he has been studying grammar. From the simplest sentence, as, The rose is fragrant, through such sentences as, Sweet is the breath of morn, and

> By cool Siloam's shady rill
> How fair the lily grows,

on to such a sentence as this,

> O'er the smooth enamelled green,
> Where no print of foot hath been,
> Follow me, as I sing
> And touch the warbled string,

the child has been solving the thought of the author before making a beginning of the grammatical analysis of the sentences. Just as two years of study given to the delightful game of checkers lays a good foundation for the solution of the more intricate problems arising on a chessboard, so this elementary study of sentence-structure gives the strength and shrewdness necessary for the analysis of the subtler and more involved structure of the mighty periods of Burke and Milton.

Very closely related to what has just been said, is a certain sentence-sense or sentence-feeling that comes along with the study of grammar. After an examination of the beautiful sentences usually found in grammars, — and no grammar has a right to consideration for a moment that does not contain beautiful thoughts couched in words of beauty, — a pupil has learned to love a sentence in which the parts are arranged in a manner perfectly adapted to the thought. This appreciation of the strong and the beautiful expression gives him real joy when he swings into the rhythmical cadences of the great masterpieces.

Moreover, this same feeling for a perfect sentence gently moulds his own expression. The hand is subdued to what it works in; and the mind surely comes to take on the beautiful form and delicate color of these wondrous creations. How could a boy who had learned to seek out the subjects and predicates of Whittier's verses write a sentence in which there was no predicate? And how could he leave a clause hanging in mid-air, if he had gained what we have called sentence-sense? Headless and bodiless members of sentences, dislocated relative clauses, dangling participles and participial phrases are impossible to a boy who has gained the feeling of a sentence, sentence-sense.

In a yet more definite manner, the study of grammar assists the work of composition; for it gives us a body of rules of great value in correcting faulty English. While it is doubtless true that many good grammarians use barbarous English and some of the artists in the use of our language have never seen a grammar, yet a man's sense of justice would be questioned if he should assert that the rules of grammar are useless as an aid to pure diction. Many a young barbarian in speech has been civilized and brought within the pale of refined society by the corrective discipline of grammar. And hosts of children of foreign parentage consider this much maligned grammar their greatest benefactor in securing them control of their adopted tongue.

Yet not for its ministry in the interpretation of literature, not for its assistance towards a correct use of our language, but for the possibilities it contains as an exercise of the reasoning faculty does grammar make its strongest plea for a place in our schools. William James in his "Psychology" (vol. ii, chap. xxii) tells us that the art of the reasoner consists of two stages : first, sagacity, or the ability to discover characteristics; and second, learning, or a knowledge of certain consequences or concomitants of the selected characteristics. Now what does the youth studying grammar do? For illustration take the easy sentence, "Sweet is the breath of morn." The boy wishes to discover what the word "Sweet" is in this sentence. What, then, are its characteristics? He discovers that it names an attribute of the subject, "the breath of morn ; " and it completes the assertion made by the verb " is." These are the two characteristics essential for his purpose, and in their discovery he has taken the first step in the process of reasoning. Next his learning tells him that an element of a sentence having the two characteristics found is called an attribute complement. Therefore " Sweet " is here an attribute complement. He has taken the second step in the process, and his reasoning is complete. This is the method used by Socrates and Plato, by Galileo and Copernicus, by Darwin and Spencer. It is the method of all thinkers.

It was because there lay hidden in language such excellent matter for developing power that those old schoolmasters set their disciples at work in Greek and Latin. Those were grand days for the intellect; and it certainly has not yet been settled that for mental discipline the new education is superior to the old. Yet our own English language has certain advantages over any inflected language. It takes but a day for a youngster to learn that a Latin noun ending in *am* is in the accusative case; but by no such simple tag can he arrive at the objective case of an English noun. It requires much more sagacity to reach such a conclusion in English. To-day, as in the days of our fathers, language — it may be Latin, Greek, German, or French, or it may be our own native tongue, the peer of any or of all — has a first place in our best schools.

In an address delivered before the students of London University on the relative value of the mental discipline to be derived from the study of language as compared with the study of science, Mr. Tyndall, one of the great scientists of all time, said : " English grammar was the most important discipline of my boyhood. The piercing through the involved and inverted sentences of 'Paradise Lost ;' the linking of the verb to its often distant nominative, of the relative to its distant antecedent, of the agent to the object of the transitive verb, of the preposition to the pronoun which it governed ; the study of variations in mood and tense, the transformations often necessary to bring out the true grammatical structure of a sentence, — all this was to my young mind a discipline óf the highest value, and, indeed, a source of unflagging delight."

In the same chapter on Reasoning, Mr. James tells us that the first step in the process is the more important and the more difficult one, — the noting of essential characteristics. It is this sagacity that differentiates geniuses, either philosophers or poets, from the common herd of men. And grammar is peculiarly fitted to train the powers of observation. It does not require a very old child to observe that hydrogen is colorless, odorless, and inflammable; that is easy. But it requires an acute observer to note that such an abstract thing as a word names an attribute of the subject, and completes the assertion made by a verb. As far as sagacity is concerned, grammar makes severer demands than the easier problems of chemistry or any other physical science. It is *par excellence* the branch in our courses of study for training the reasoning power. In our mental gymnasiums, for developing quick, accurate, sure-footed thinkers, no equipment has yet been discovered to displace the study of grammar.

These, then, are the reasons for studying grammar: it gives a student the power to unravel the intricate web of thought exhibited in our great, beautiful literature; it cultivates in him a certain sentence-sense which instantly recognizes harmony and loveliness and strength in the work of the masters, and which guards him against any possible mutilated and misshapen products of his own composition; and it develops thinkers, men who can analyze conditions and separate the essential from the non-essential, men who can see through the masses of things to their ultimate consequences.

Assuming that the main purpose of the study of grammar is the development of the reasoning faculty leads to a few suggestions concerning definitions. To give training in careful thinking, classifications must be strictly scientific; definitions must be accurate. The requisites of a good definition are : first, it must include all members of its class ; second, it must exclude all members not of its class; and third, it must be simple and brief. Definitions are always hard to frame; and if they fulfill the first two requirements, they sometimes cannot be brief and simple. Then the question arises, which shall be sacrificed? Shall it be accuracy or simplicity, truth or brevity? To illustrate, a pronoun is sometimes defined as a word used instead of a noun. This is simple and brief; but is it correct? In the sentences, To be honest under all circumstances is difficult, but *it* pays ; *Who* steals *my* purse steals trash ; *Who* is the King of Glory? the italicized words are called pronouns by all, yet not one of them stands for a noun. The definition fails in the first requisite; it does not include some members of its class. This is like defining reptiles as scaly creatures that crawl on their bellies without the use of limbs. To be sure, all such creatures are reptiles; but there are a lot of other creatures besides snakes included under the term reptiles. Alligators, lizards, and tortoises are reptiles; and no zoölogist would allow a student to give such an imperfect definition. Then to avoid this difficulty, some grammars say

that a word used instead of a noun is a pronoun.
This statement is true; but the unfortunate thing
about it is that the child, and sometimes the
teacher, too, is misled into the belief that he has
learned a definition of a pronoun. It is like saying, all scaly creatures crawling on their bellies
without the use of limbs are reptiles. Such a statement is true; but it is not a definition of reptiles,
for alligators, lizards, and tortoises — all of them
reptiles — do use limbs in crawling. Moreover, a
definition may include too much; as, an objective
complement is a word that names an attribute
of the object. This would include a great many
words which no one would call objective complements; and so it fails in the second requisite of a
good definition. If the main purpose in teaching
grammar is to make close, careful thinkers, definitions must be used that do actually define, that
really do classify.

It is a well-established principle of pedagogy
that there is a waste of mental energy whenever a
fact has to be un-learned and then re-learned, because the first statement of it was incorrect. That
first statement persists, and rough handling is
needed to bring it under. For this reason correct
definitions, so far as possible, should be learned at
once and for all. It is true that incomplete definitions of some grammatical elements are given in

most language books. These are all that the children of the lower grades can comprehend. But when the real study of grammar begins, inaccurate, tentative definitions should be dismissed; and complete definitions, definitions that will stand the test of the advanced work in the high school and college, should be learned.

From what has been said it may be inferred that grammar is a hard subject. It is, — it certainly is no subject for babes. At one time it was thought that the study could be begun in the third grade; now by an all but universal custom it is deferred to the seventh grade, and there are some who would place it even later. Learning to read and write, to express in straightforward English his own simple thoughts, and to handle simple numbers; acquiring manual skill; gathering a few facts concerning this great, beautiful world about him; laying away in memory's treasure-box some glorious gems from our history and literature, — these are tasks enough for any child during the first six years of his school life.

Of the difficulties in the study of grammar, some have to be faced at the very beginning, and others can be delayed to a later day. Of the former the most troublesome is the separation of a sentence into its simple elements, and especially the analysis of the predicate. Of the latter are the subjunctive mood and the use of some of our common verbs, such as *shall, will, may, can,* and so forth.

Right here some persons ask, if analysis is so hard, why begin with it? Why not begin with the parts of speech? While it is doubtless true that many words, single and alone, may be classified as name-words, or nouns, and action-words, or verbs, yet a child would not go far before he discovered that his basis for classification was imperfect. If the chief purpose of grammar is the development of the power to reason correctly, any hap-hazard classification can find no place in a text-book. A word belongs to a definite class because it performs a certain function in the sentence. Function is the basis of classification in grammar, and the function of a word must be determined by its use in a sentence. Analysis, then, must come before there can be any accurate classification of the parts of speech; it must stand at the beginning of any logical grammar.

It will be helpful to consider for a short time the difficulties that must be met at the very beginning of the study of grammar.

A sentence is usually defined as the expression of a complete thought. Now what comprises a complete thought? Possibly this can be most easily answered by observing a child just learning to talk. The first words a child says are names of things that interest him.   These names do not express a complete thought, though there may be in the child's mind some thought about the objects he names.   Next he passes to another group of words, attributes.   Holding tight in his sticky fist a piece of striped candy, he says "Sweet."   Possibly Rover warns off a stranger, and he says "Bark."   Soon he begins to combine subject and attribute, and says, "Candy — sweet" or "Rover — bark."   He has used the two most important elements of every sentence.   In his own mind these two elements are joined, the attribute is asserted of the subject; and it will not be many weeks before the little fellow will express this relation in complete sentences, "Candy is sweet," "Rover barks."   Grown people and even children of the seventh grade have come so far on the language road that they have forgotten how simple the beginnings are.   Yet in every thought, no matter how complex, there will be found those three simple elements, — subject, predicate attribute, and copula.

Two facts about this simple predicate should be noted.   Had the candy been put on the table by a designing mother, the child would have run to her saying, "Candy — on the table."   In this, just as in "Candy — sweet," the child uses subject and predicate attribute. In the former sentence the attribute named by the child was a quality of the candy; in the latter it is the location of the candy. The first fact about this simple predicate is that a word denoting quality is not the only attribute; it may be a phrase, as in this sentence, or it may be a clause, examples of which may be found in all grammars.

The second fact is that the asserting word and the attribute are often combined in one. When the child says, " Rover barks," he means to unite his idea of barking with his idea of Rover, just as he did when he said " Rover — bark." The copula and the attribute are compressed into one word, "barks." The elements of a thought are always subject, predicate attribute, and copula; but very frequently the copula and attribute are expressed by one element of a sentence.

Two other elements are sometimes found in a predicate, — an object complement and an objective complement. The former is usually easy for children, but the latter may need some explanation. Possibly the term will be better understood from illustration.

   1. James saw the kettle, black and sooty.
   2. James thought the kettle black and sooty.
   3. James made the kettle black and sooty.

In all three sentences, " black and sooty " are attributes of " kettle." Yet they have not the same use in any two of the sentences. The first sentence means, James saw the black and sooty kettle. The second means James thought the kettle to be black and sooty. In this " black and sooty " are attribute complements used after *to be* understood, serving as copula. In the third sentence, the words " black and sooty " name attributes of " kettle ; " but they have this peculiar characteristic: these attributes are the result of the action asserted by the verb. This last is the distinguishing characteristic of an objective complement: it names an attribute that was caused by the action asserted by the verb. In a lesson on objective complements, it would be well to find, first, all the object complements ; next, all the words naming attributes of these objects ; and, third, select from these last all those that name attributes resulting from the action asserted by the verb. These words are objective complements.

The study of these five elements of a sentence, — subject, predicate attribute, object complement, objective complement, and copula, — together with the recognition of nouns, verbs, and the easier pronouns, makes enough for the first term's work in grammar. Any haste over this part of the work will only cause delay later ; and it may be safely affirmed that a clear understanding of these elements of sentences makes the remaining work simple. The second term will be employed principally with modifiers, — words, phrases, and clauses,

— introducing the kinds of sentences, and with a recognition of the other parts of speech. The second year will be devoted to a detailed study of the parts of speech and their modifications. These time suggestions are made for classes beginning this study in the seventh grade; should this work be taken up later, the time for completing it will be shorter, but the relative amount of time will not be much changed.

In view of the threefold purpose for which grammar is studied, some suggestions as to method may be appropriate. All study of sentences, whatever its nature, fosters an ability to look through their meaning, and so is a valuable aid in the study of literature. So, too, during all the time given to grammar, the student is gaining a sentence-sense, valuable in both literature and composition. These advantages, however, are mainly incidental. But for the correction of errors in expression, it is well to have definite exercises. When pupils have learned in grammar the principles they are breaking in their common speech, it is time to devise exercises for special purposes. Incorrect sentences for correction should not be made up, but they should be selected from the daily world of the pupils. Each error should be pointed out, corrected, and the grammatical principle demanding the change should be fully stated. If needed, one exercise a week in the second year of the study may profitably be given to this work. And to do this will not be to deprive technical grammar of any time; for beside the eradication of numerous errors, as much grammatical knowledge is fixed in this as in any other way.

This, however, is but a small part of the work of grammar. By far the most time will be given to the analysis of sentences and to the classification and modifications of the parts of speech. What is the best way to study in order to serve the high purpose for which it is taught?

Not many years ago the method was at least simple and uniform. It consisted of a definition, an illustration, and a group of sentences for practice. Commencing with the group of sentences for practice, what do we usually find? That the whole number are made on exactly the same model. A boy would have little of the New England Yankee in his blood who could not make an eighty per cent guess on such a lesson. The conditions are the same as we often see in algebra. The rule for a case is given, then follows a group of examples every one of which is solved in exactly the same way. Such an arrangement requires little or no sagacity. The real test in algebra, as in grammar, comes when the child is called upon to observe the features of his problem in order to tell what class

it belongs to.   All exercises should contain a suffi-
cient number of examples to illustrate the special
case; but there should be mixed with them enough
problems of kinds previously studied to demand
something more than parrot-work, — to require
sagacity, to tax the powers of observation.

Again, even among the sentences that are given
for illustration of a principle, there should be the
greatest possible variety.   If the lesson is on
adverbial nouns, and every sentence is arranged
in the same order, — subject, verb, and adverbial
objective, — it can be learned with the least possible effort.   The ordinary boy can throw it off
while busy at some new play for his football team;
and as far as giving him power is concerned, the
football problem has a much better claim to his
time.   The only way to get thinking is to demand
thinking.   Variety, endless variety, — this it is
which calls upon the lad to bend all his energy
to his work; this it is that demands and yields
in return sagacity, the peculiar endowment of
geniuses.

Once more, the part of reasoning which requires the greatest sagacity is not the recognition
of classes after classification has been made, but
the observation of like qualities by which objects
may be classified.   After he has been told what it
is, almost any child can recognize a quadrilateral

when he sees it; but he must have some sagacity
if, when he sees drawn on a board a rhombus, a
trapezium, a trapezoid, and a rectangle, he can
select the one characteristic by which all these may
be included in one class, and so derive his definition of a quadrilateral. For thousands of years
men had seen apples, the moon, earth, and sun;
yet Newton was the first to see in these a likeness
that led him to the law of gravitation. In grammar some of the best work can be done before the
new classification has been made and the definition
has been formulated. A large variety of sentences
containing the new thing should be submitted, and
from this multitude of examples the one like characteristic should be sought out as it was with the
geometrical figures. After the peculiar characteristics of this new thing are discovered, the pupils
are ready to formulate their definition. In the
German schools, where we American teachers may
yet learn a few things, all grammar of their native
tongue is derived in this way, their histories and
literature furnishing the material for the examples.
This part of a grammar exercise is invaluable, yet
this part is omitted from many text-books. It is
only here that the child is taught to reason induc-
tively, the process by which new worlds are discovered and new inventions are made.

Grammar is then first and foremost a reasoning

subject. No other branch in our course of study sets such fine problems. What an opportunity for his keenest wits when the boy meets for the first time these sentences: I have three dollars; The sled cost three dollars; and he is set to determine the use of the word "dollars"! What joy illumines his face when he finds that in spite of their appearance so like, there is one essential difference, and that they are not at all the same thing! And when he arrives at the discussion of some common verbs, he has entered a field that will require his keenest powers of discrimination. In such sentences as these: I shall go if it is clear; and I shall go, mother, no matter what you say, he is called upon to determine just what is asserted. Is it the going, or is it determination, even obstinacy? The answer to this question will decide whether "shall go" is a verb-phrase, or "shall" alone is a verb. Here is a test that will demand the quickest wits, the clearest eye, the surest aim; and who wins here has a right to the title of champion.

A word of caution should be spoken to the teacher. Don't be in a hurry. The facts of grammar are not of great value; the training from its study is invaluable. Be in no haste; and know that if the foundation has been well put down, the superstructure will rise surely and safely, a thing of beauty and a cause of rejoicing. The words most often on your lips will be, "Take time to think," "That is not careful thinking," "That seems reasonable;" for the end always before you — is the cultivation of thought-power. And know, too, that when you teach grammar in this way, you are training youth to a strength that may speak like Webster, sing like Lowell, invent like Edison, and conquer new worlds of commerce as Americans.

WILLIAM FRANK WEBSTER.

MINNEAPOLIS, MINN., February 1, 1905.

The principles and methods outlined in the above paper have been carefully worked out by Mr. Webster in "The Elements of English Grammar," a school text-book recently published by us. See third cover page.

HOUGHTON, MIFFLIN & CO.

THE WEBSTER–COOLEY LANGUAGE SERIES

A complete and successful course in English for intermediate, grammar, and high school grades by W. F. Webster and Alice Woodworth Cooley.

FOR INTERMEDIATE GRADES

Cooley's Language Lessons from Literature, Book I, 45 cents
Cooley's Language Lessons from Literature, Book II, 65 cents
Book II, also in two parts, each, 45 cents

FOR GRAMMAR OR HIGH SCHOOL GRADES

Webster's Elements of English Grammar   50 cents
Webster's Elementary Composition   65 cents

FOR HIGH SCHOOL GRADES

Webster's English : Composition and Literature   90 cents

NOTE : — Language Lessons from Literature, Book II, is planned to cover two years' work. For the convenience of schools which prefer a separate book for each grade, it is also published in two parts (as stated above) each covering a year's work.

Correspondence with a view to examination and adoption of these books is solicited by the publishers.

HOUGHTON, MIFFLIN & COMPANY

4 PARK STREET, BOSTON ; 85 FIFTH AVENUE, NEW YORK ;
378–388 WABASH AVENUE, CHICAGO.